Castletown School, Caithness

WORLD ABOUT US

TRAFFIC POLLUTION

M. BRIGHT

GLOUCESTER PRESS
London · New York · Toronto · Sydney

© Aladdin Books Ltd 1991

Designed and produced by
Aladdin Books Ltd
28 Percy Street
London W1P 9FF

First published in
Great Britain in 1991 by
Franklin Watts Ltd
96 Leonard Street
London EC2A 4RH

Design: David West
Children's
Book Design
Editor: Fiona Robertson
Illustrator: Simon Bishop
Consultant: Malcolm Fergusson

ISBN 0 7496 0684 3

Printed in Belgium

Contents

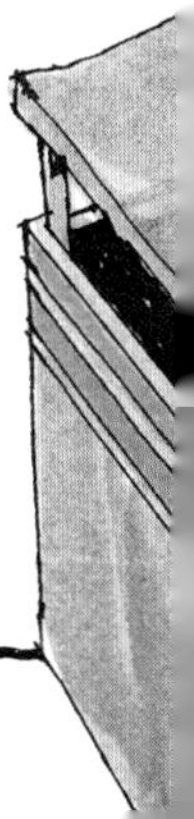

Introduction

There are 400 million cars, lorries and buses in the world today. By the year 2000, there will be 700 million. More and more people now depend on vehicles, both for travelling and for transporting goods. However, there is a price to pay. As the number of vehicles goes up, so too does the amount of pollution produced. This can have serious effects both on the environment and on our health.

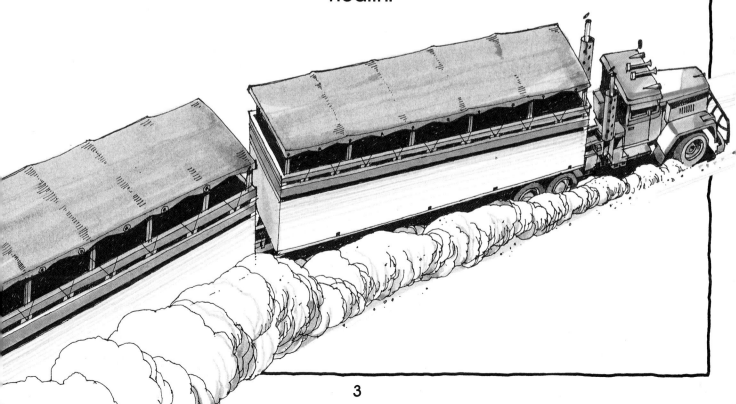

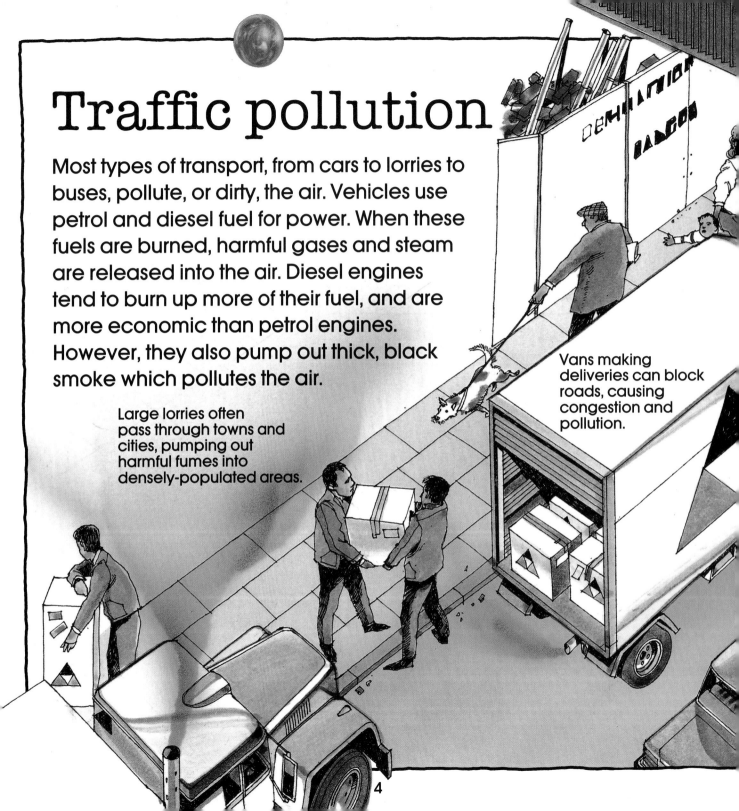

Traffic pollution

Most types of transport, from cars to lorries to buses, pollute, or dirty, the air. Vehicles use petrol and diesel fuel for power. When these fuels are burned, harmful gases and steam are released into the air. Diesel engines tend to burn up more of their fuel, and are more economic than petrol engines. However, they also pump out thick, black smoke which pollutes the air.

Large lorries often pass through towns and cities, pumping out harmful fumes into densely-populated areas.

Vans making deliveries can block roads, causing congestion and pollution.

Heavy build-up of traffic in towns and cities raises the noise level to unpleasant, even harmful levels.

Cars used for short private journeys are often the most wasteful.

How cars pollute

The petrol and diesel oil burned by cars, lorries, and buses are a complex mixture of hydrocarbons (chemicals made up of carbon and hydrogen only). When mixed with air in an engine, they burn producing harmful gases and tiny droplets of unburned hydrocarbons. Lead can also get into the air from exhaust fumes.

The figures below show how much of the pollution in the air is produced by cars.

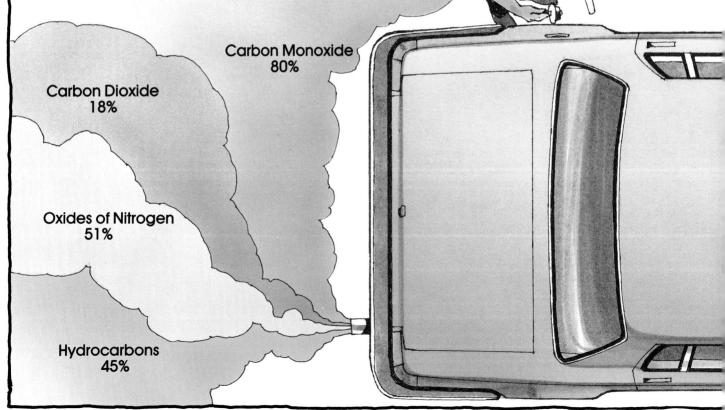

Carbon Monoxide
80%

Carbon Dioxide
18%

Oxides of Nitrogen
51%

Hydrocarbons
45%

Lead is added to petrol in many countries to make it run through the engine more smoothly. However, lead is harmful to people's health and to the environment.

Exhaust fumes

Carbon dioxide, carbon monoxide and steam are given out when fuel is burned. All of these are greenhouse gases, which means they make the air warmer. Nitrogen oxides are also released in exhaust fumes and help to form acid rain.

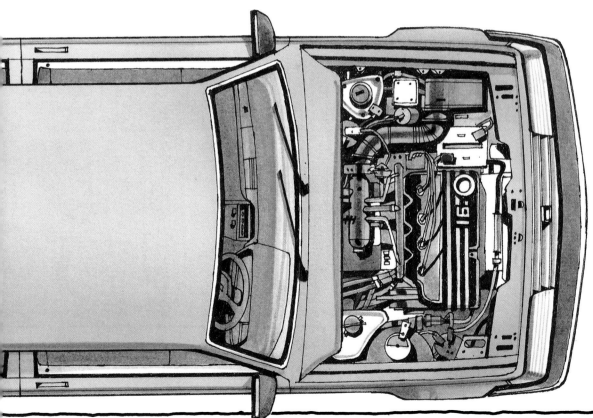

About 85 per cent of the energy used by vehicles is wasted; it ends up heating the air.

In towns and cities

In built-up areas, such as towns and cities, air pollution levels can be especially bad. The pollution from car exhausts is made worse by the gases which come from factories and power stations. Buildings restrict the flow of wind, which stops the pollution from clearing. Similarly, polluted air is often trapped at low levels by mountains or valleys. Air pollution in these areas can reach very high levels.

The air over major cities is often clouded by pollution, mainly from vehicles and industry.

Dirt from traffic

The smoke and grime from cars and lorries not only pollute the air; they can also make buildings dirty. Acid rain, which is partly caused by exhaust fumes, can also eat into stone and destroy buildings and statues.

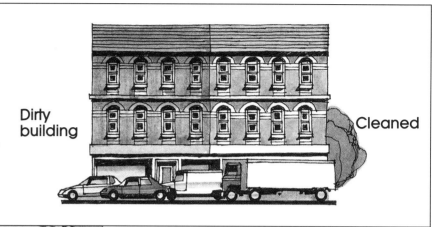

Dirty building

Cleaned

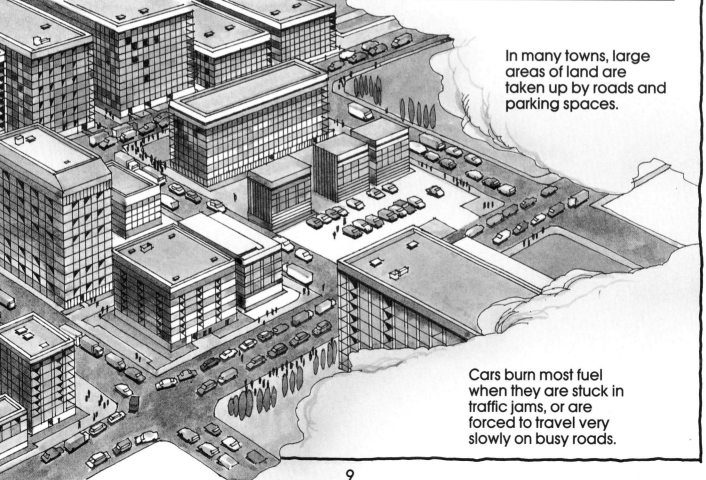

In many towns, large areas of land are taken up by roads and parking spaces.

Cars burn most fuel when they are stuck in traffic jams, or are forced to travel very slowly on busy roads.

In the country

Fields, forests, crops and animals near a busy road or motorway all suffer from the effects of traffic pollution. The gases and lead in exhaust fumes can poison crops and be dangerous to animals that breathe them in. Building new roads cuts through the countryside and destroys the homes of plants and animals living there.

A single motorway lane takes up the same space as a single railway line. But the railway line transports up to ten times more people and causes far less pollution.

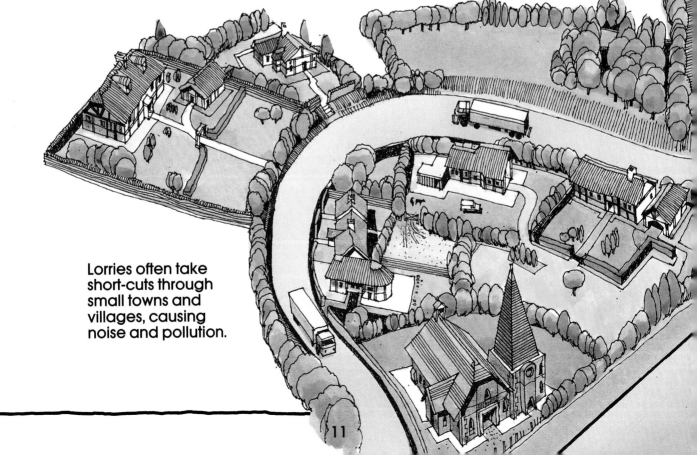

Lorries often take short-cuts through small towns and villages, causing noise and pollution.

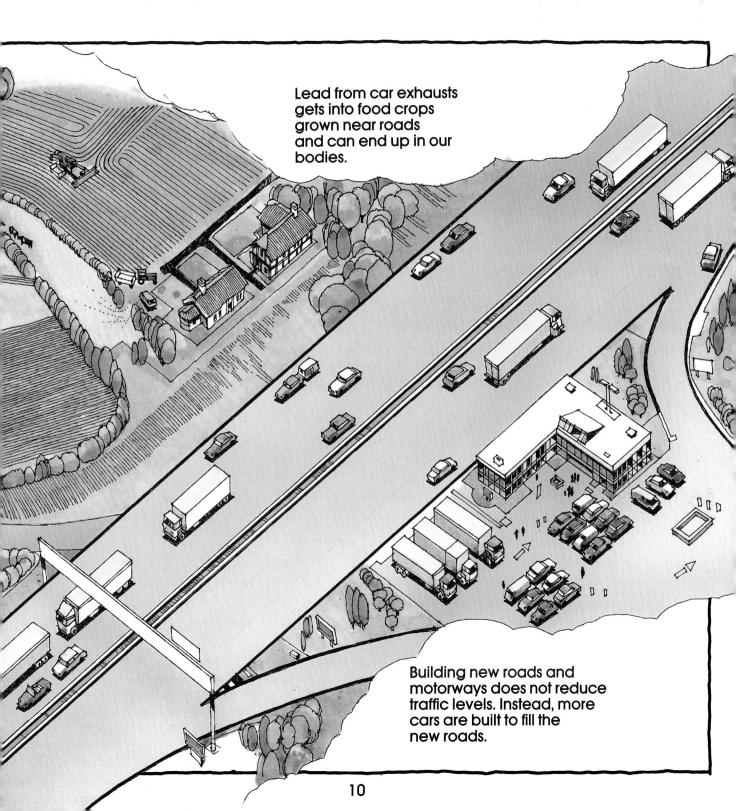

Lead from car exhausts gets into food crops grown near roads and can end up in our bodies.

Building new roads and motorways does not reduce traffic levels. Instead, more cars are built to fill the new roads.

The effects

The nitrogen oxides in exhaust fumes mix with the water in clouds to make very weak nitric acid. This acid then falls to the ground with rain and is called acid rain. Acid rain is harmful to plant and animal life. Carbon dioxide is a greenhouse gas which traps heat close to the Earth's surface. If too much heat is trapped, temperatures around the world could go up.

In some cities the pollution is so bad that people have to wear masks or stay indoors.

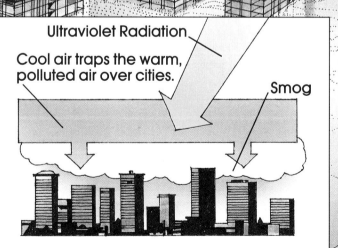

Smog

When hydrocarbons and nitrogen oxides mix with strong sunlight, ozone is made. Near the ground ozone forms an evil-smelling and poisonous smog, called photo-chemical smog. Ozone is also a greenhouse gas.

Ultraviolet Radiation

Cool air traps the warm, polluted air over cities.

Smog

High up in the sky, ozone protects the Earth from the Sun's harmful ultraviolet rays.

At ground level, ozone kills trees, causes metal to rot, or corrode, and rubber to crack. Smogs containing ozone are often bluish in colour.

Reducing the amount of traffic on the street is the best way to cut down on noise pollution.

Noise nuisance

People living and working close to heavy traffic can suffer headaches and even permanent damage to their hearing because of the noise from vehicle engines. In addition, the vibrations caused by heavy lorries or buses in towns and villages make cracks appear in buildings. Road surfaces may also be affected.

The foundation of old, historic buildings are most at risk from the vibrations of heavy lorries.

Health threats

The pollution which comes from cars not only affects the atmosphere, it can threaten our health, too. Smog and other air pollutants can cause skin irritations and breathing problems like asthma, and also affect the eyes, nose and throat. The lead in exhaust fumes can damage the kidneys and the nervous system.

Carbon monoxide stops the body from taking in enough oxygen. People feel tired and cannot think or act quickly.

Dirt and grime in the air can get into people's eyes and may cause skin irritations.

Tiny particles of unburned carbon – called particulates – are given out when diesel is burned. They are suspected of causing cancer.

Very high levels of lead in the air are harmful to pregnant women, and can also stop young children's brains from developing properly.

Worldwide problems

Many wealthy countries, like Britain and the United States, are now taking action to clean up traffic pollution levels. However, most poorer countries cannot afford to reduce pollution. Their cars are often older and inefficient and the level of lead in the fuel is high. This makes the air pollution caused by traffic much worse.

Cars in poorer countries are not built with the latest technology. Many of them cannot use devices like catalytic converters, and so traffic pollution will continue to be a problem in the future.

In poorer countries, most people travel on foot, or by bicycle or public transport. If all these people were to own cars, the effects on the environment would be catastrophic.

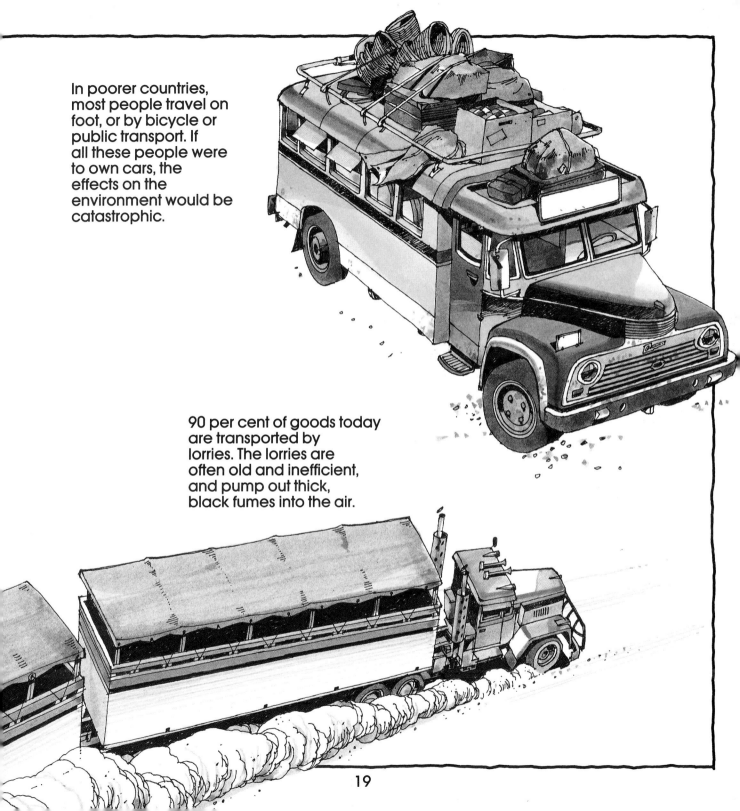

90 per cent of goods today are transported by lorries. The lorries are often old and inefficient, and pump out thick, black fumes into the air.

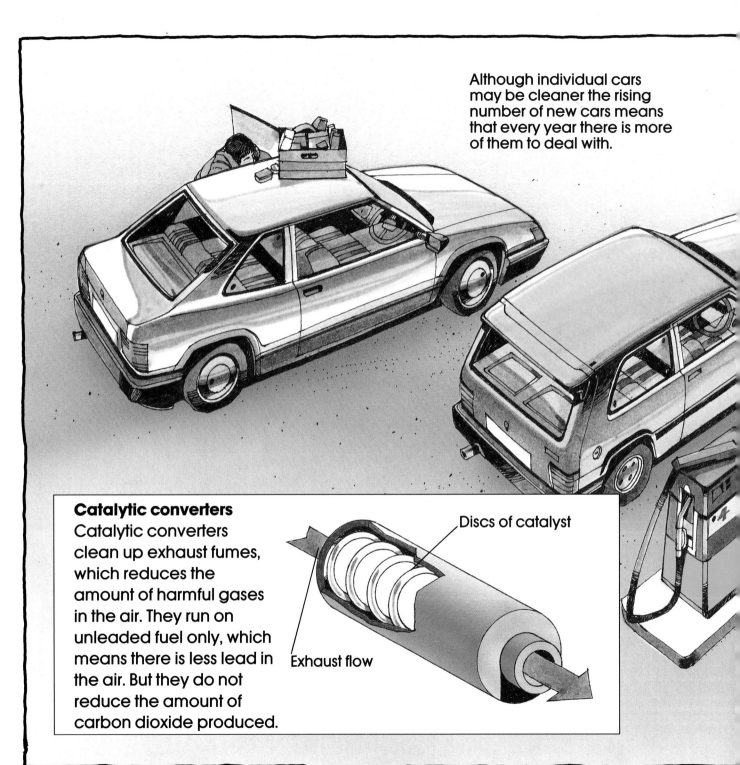

Although individual cars may be cleaner the rising number of new cars means that every year there is more of them to deal with.

Catalytic converters

Catalytic converters clean up exhaust fumes, which reduces the amount of harmful gases in the air. They run on unleaded fuel only, which means there is less lead in the air. But they do not reduce the amount of carbon dioxide produced.

Discs of catalyst

Exhaust flow

Energy savers

As the number of vehicles continues to increase, research is being carried out into making their engines more efficient. Building cars with lighter materials makes them easier to move and wastes less energy. Fuel efficiency can also be improved by making vehicles more streamlined, or aerodynamic. This reduces their resistance to wind.

Unleaded fuel is now widely available in Europe and North America. Catalytic converters can only use unleaded fuel, so most newer cars run on unleaded only.

Millions of tonnes of oil are burned every year as petrol or diesel. Oil is a fossil fuel, and eventually supplies will run out. Making engines more efficient will protect energy supplies for the future.

Alternatives

As pollution problems from burning petrol increase, a number of alternative fuels are being tested. Ethanol, which is made from sugar cane, hydrogen and natural gas all have problems at present, but are being researched for use in the future. Similarly, the electric car is a possibility. Modern batteries are powerful enough, but are very heavy and need constant recharging.

Hydrogen (shown right) does not produce pollution when burned, only water vapour. However, liquid hydrogen takes a lot of energy to produce and must be stored at very low temperatures.

Cars can be specially shaped to allow air to flow over them smoothly. This improves the car's speed and performance.

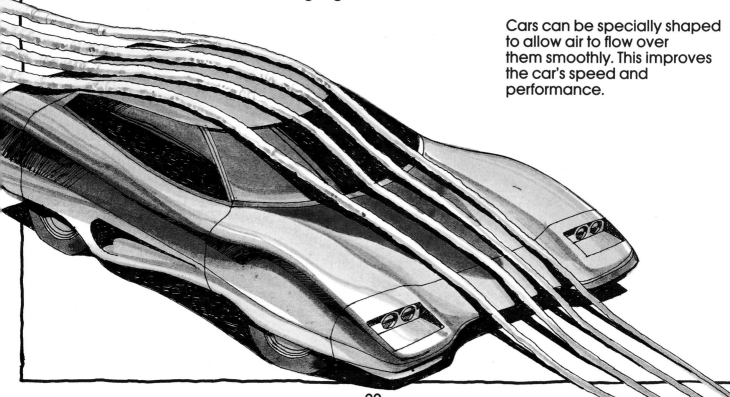

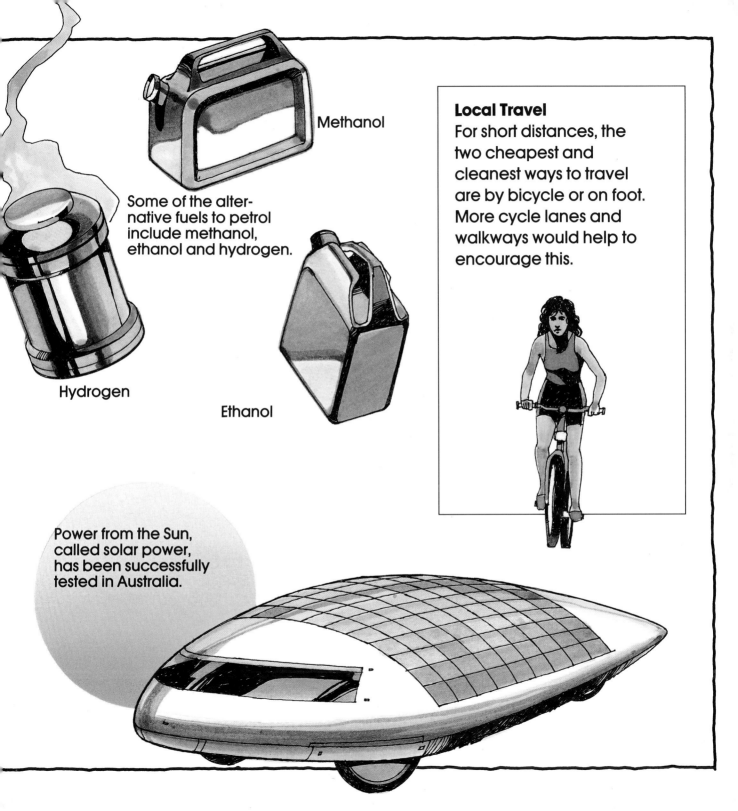

Methanol

Some of the alter-
native fuels to petrol
include methanol,
ethanol and hydrogen.

Hydrogen

Ethanol

Local Travel
For short distances, the
two cheapest and
cleanest ways to travel
are by bicycle or on foot.
More cycle lanes and
walkways would help to
encourage this.

Power from the Sun,
called solar power,
has been successfully
tested in Australia.

A breath of fresh air

Most cities today are choked by traffic and filled with the exhaust fumes from cars and lorries. Public transport is often crowded and not reliable.

City filled with traffic and pollution

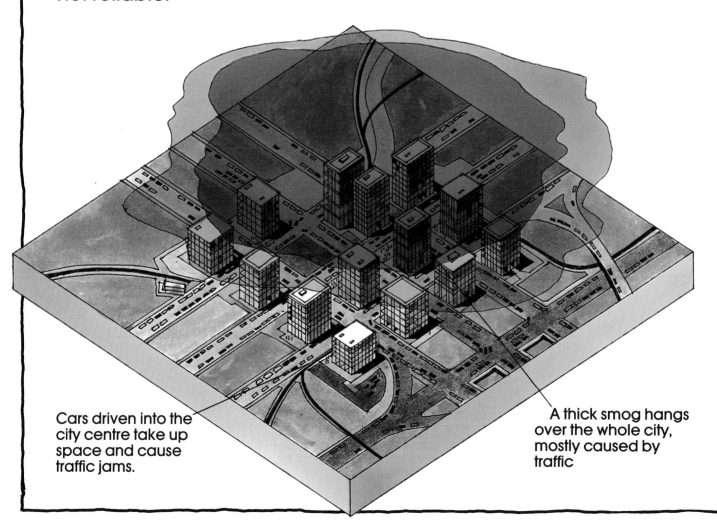

Cars driven into the city centre take up space and cause traffic jams.

A thick smog hangs over the whole city, mostly caused by traffic

Cleaner cities could be made possible by banning cars and lorries from city centres. Shopping and office areas would be restricted for pedestrians only. More efficient public transportation, with buses, trains, and electric trams would be available.

The solution to pollution

Motorists leave their vehicles outside the town or city and travel in by public transport.

The centre is restricted to public transport, people on foot and delivery vehicles. There are also more cycle lanes.

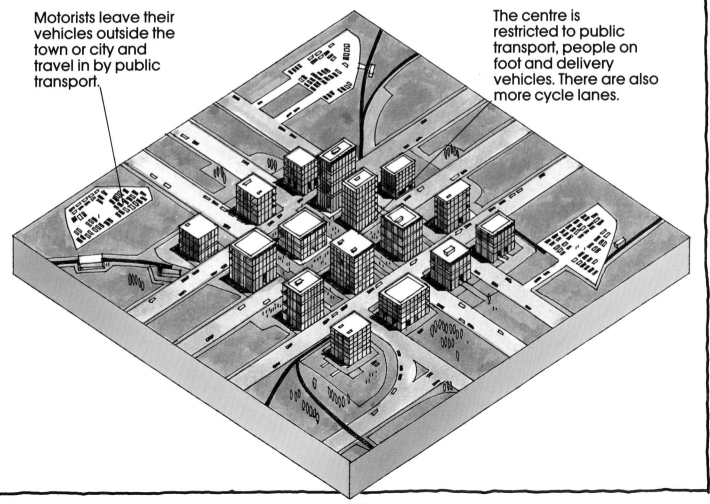

Taking action

In many cities, restrictions are being introduced to control the amount of traffic in busy city centres. Traffic has been banned from the centre of Florence, in Italy, during the day. Enforcing speed limits cuts down on the amount of fuel being wasted. These and other measures must be taken if the effects of traffic pollution are to be reduced.

Smaller cars take less materials to build and use less fuel to run.

Building cars with materials that can be recycled, saves money and energy. It also reduces the waste problems created by piles of old cars and tyres left on scrapheaps.

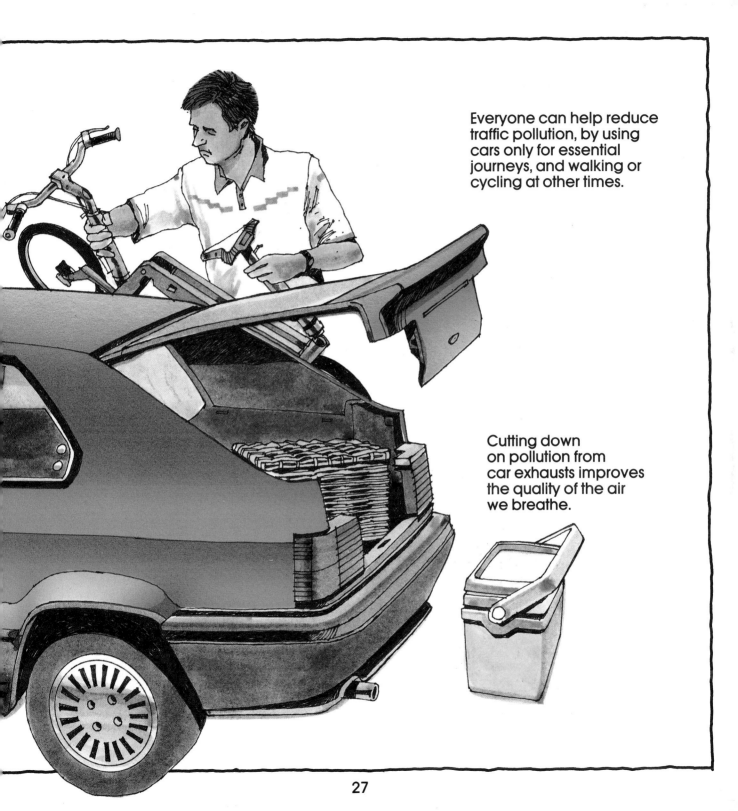

Everyone can help reduce traffic pollution, by using cars only for essential journeys, and walking or cycling at other times.

Cutting down on pollution from car exhausts improves the quality of the air we breathe.

Did you know?

Lead in the air
Before the introduction of unleaded petrol, lead in the air was a serious health threat. In Britain many crops were contaminated by the lead in the air. In the United States, a quarter of young children were exposed to lead levels high enough to affect brain development.

Losing treasures
Acid rain caused by traffic pollution has made the marble from the Parthenon in Athens wear away more in the past two decades than in the past two thousand years. Similarly, pollution from cars is destroying the Coliseum in Rome and Westminster Abbey in London.

Industry in the city

In Bombay, Beijing and Mexico City, traffic pollution adds to that from industry. Near São Paulo in Brazil lies the "Valley of Death" where pollution from factories, cars and lorries is trapped over low-lying towns and villages. Local children must visit clinics and breathe specially cleaned air in order to survive.

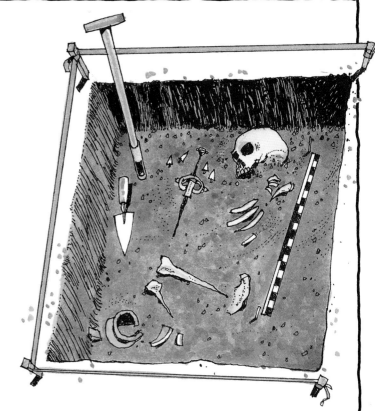

Lead: the past and the present

Peruvian skeletons over 2,700 years old have been found with lead levels a thousandth of those considered normal today. In the remote Himalayan Mountains, villagers unexposed to cars have blood lead levels that are six times less than those of people living in cities.

Polluted Olympics

The 23rd Olympic Games in 1984 were held in Los Angeles, a city filled with cars and surrounded by mountains. Strong sunlight mixes with the pollution produced to make poisonous photochemical smogs. An eagle which was the symbol of the Olympics died during the Games because of the pollution.

Catalytic converters

Since 1975, catalytic converters, or catalysts, have been fitted to all new cars in the United States. Most petrol there is now unleaded. Catalysts have cut the amount of carbon monoxide from new cars by 76 per cent. Hydrocarbons and nitrogen oxides in the air have gone down by an enormous 96 per cent.

Glossary

Acid rain
Water in the air mixes with the pollution from cars and industry to make acids which fall to the ground with rain.

Carbon dioxide
A gas found naturally in the air. Carbon dioxide helps to keep the Earth warm, and is vital to life. If too much carbon dioxide is trapped, however, temperatures could go up.

Carbon monoxide
A colourless, poisonous gas made when petrol is burned.

Fossil fuels
Coal, oil and natural gas, which come from the remains of living things, like plants and animals, which have been trapped or buried in the ground for millions of years. When burned, they release energy.

Ozone
A colourless gas which forms the protective ozone layer in the atmosphere and stops harmful ultraviolet light getting to Earth. At ground level it is poisonous.

Photochemical smog
When hydrocarbons and nitrogen oxides from vehicle exhausts mix with sunshine they form a poisonous smog containing ozone.

Resources
Anything that is useful. Natural resources include oil, wood and coal. Supplies are limited and will eventually run out.

Index

PRINTED IN BELGIUM BY
proost
INTERNATIONAL BOOK PRODUCTION